BRIGHT SHENG

TWO FOLK SONGS FROM QINGHAI

for Chorus (SATB), Percussion (2 players), and Two Pianos

(score and parts)

ED 3932

First Printing: September 1996

ISBN 978-0-7935-6778-2

G. SCHIRMER, Inc.

DISTRIBUTED BY
HAL•LEONARD® CORPORATION
7777 W. BLUEMOUND RD. P.O. BOX 13819 MILWAUKEE, WI 53213

山丹丹

I. Morningstar Lily

*Shan Dan Dan Hua (Ya) Kai Zai Ya Shong,
山　丹　丹　花（呀）開　在　崖　上，

The Morningstar Lily is in full bloom
  up on the cliff,

Gu Gu Nee Zhai Ha (Hei Ya Lee)
哥　哥　你　摘　下（嘿　呀　嘿）

My love, I will wear it

Nee Nee Nao (A Jou) Dei Shong Liao(Ya).
妹　妹　我（啊　就）戴　上　　了（呀）。

If you bring it down.

Shan Dan Dan Hua (Ya) Kai Zai Ya Shong,
山　丹　丹　花（呀）開　在　崖　上，

The morningstar lily is in full bloom
  up on the cliff,

Nee Nee Yao Dei Shong (Hei Ya Lee)
妹　妹　要　戴　上（嘿　呀　哩）

My love, if you wear it

Gu Gu Nao Zhai (A Jou) Zhai Ha.
哥　哥　我　摘（啊　就）摘　下。

I am bringing it down.

一對騾子

II. A Pair of Mules

Yee Dui Dee (Ma Jou) Luo Zi (Zhe)
一　對　的（嗎　就）騾　子（者）

Carrying a bundle of hemp,

Zou (Dee) Ning Xia (Yo),
走　（的）寧　夏（喲），

A pair of mules are going to Ning-Xia,

Tuo (Ei) Yee Kun Ma (Yo),
馱（哎）一　捆　麻（喲），

Hui Lai Shi (Ma Jou) Shao Liao Dai
回　來　時（嗎　就）捎　了　袋

When they are back,

Zao (Ya Ha Jou) Er,
棗（呀　哈　就）兒，

They will bring a sack of jujube (Chinese
  date).

(Dian Dian Hua Er Kai Ya Yo).
（點　點　花　兒　開　呀　喲）。

* The Ping Ying pronunciation is based on the Qinghai dialect of China.

PRONUNCIATION GUIDE

(Consonants and vowels of the Chinese Phonetic Alphabet and their corresponding International Phonetic Symbols)

CPA	IPS	CPA	IPS	CPA	IPS	CPA	IPS
b	ɓ	zh	tʂ	ai	ai	iong	yŋ
p	p'	ch	tʂ'	ei	ei	ua	ua
m	m	sh	ʂ	ao	au	uo	uə
f	f	r	ʐ	ou	əu	uai	uai
d	t			an	an	ui, uei	uei
t	t'	y	j	en	ən	uan	uan
n	n	w	w	ang	aŋ	un, uen	uən
l	l			eng	əŋ	uang	uaŋ
g	k	a	a	ong	uŋ	üe	yɛ
k	k'	o	o	ia	ia	üan	yan
h	x	e	ə	ie	iɛ	ün	yn
j	tɕ	i	i	iao	iau		
q	tɕ'	u	u	iu, iou	iəu		
x	ɕ	ü	y	ian	ian		
z	ts	-i	ɿ (ʅ)*	in	in		
c	ts'	êa	ɛ	iang	iaŋ		
s	s	-er	ər	ing	iŋ		

* ɿ after zcs, ʅ after zh, ch, sh, and r.

PROGRAM NOTE

Two Folk Songs from Qinghai begins with "Morningstar Lily," a happy and joyous love song that bears the subtitle, "Homage to Igor Stravinsky." The second, "A Pair of Mules (Homage to Ferde Grofé)," is the more intense of the two, the homage referring to the wood block "horses" of the *Grand Canyon Suite*. The journey from Qinghai to Ning-Xia is very difficult with mules—it takes days. There are dangerous gorges, the wind blows hard, and the mountainous road is slippery in the rain. I was partly thinking that, after such a journey, you acquire a sense of achievement.

—BRIGHT SHENG

Two Folk Songs from Qinghai can also be performed in a version for chorus and orchestra. The instrumentation for the orchestral version is:

Flute (Piccolo)
Oboe
Clarinet in A
Bassoon

2 Horns in F
Trumpet in C
Trombone

Percussion (2 players)*
Timpani, Crotales, Marimba, Small Tambourine, Wood Blocks,
Finger Cymbal, Small Sizzle Cymbal, Small Tamtam

Piano

Strings

*The percussion parts are the same for both the orchestral and chamber versions.

duration: ca. 10 minutes

The orchestra version of Two Folk Songs from Qinghai *was commissioned by the John Oliver Chorale and Orchestra, who gave the premiere performance of the first movement in 1991. The full work was premiered by Gerard Schwarz with the Seattle Symphony on March 2, 1991.*

premiere performance: March 21, 1992, Dessoff Choirs, Amy Kaiser conductor, Merkin Concert Hall, New York City

Performance material (for the orchestra version) is available on rental from the publisher.

TWO FOLK SONGS FROM QINGHAI

I. Morningstar Lily
(Homage to Igor Stravinsky)

山丹丹

Bright Sheng
(1990)

Hei Ya Lee Mee Mee Nao A Jou Dei Shong, Dei Shong.
Hei Ya Lee Mee Mee Nao A Jou Mee Mee Jou Dei Shong Liao Mee Mee Jou Dei Shong Liao.
Hei Hei Ya
Hei Hei Ya

Hei Ya   Hei   Hei Ya   Hei Ya Lee   Hei Ya
Hei Ya   Hei   Hei Ya   Hei Ya Lee   Hei Ya
Shan Dan Dan Hua   Ya   Kai Zai Ya   Shong,   Mee Mee Yao Dei Shong   Hei Ya   Lee
Shan Dan Dan Hua   Ya   Kai Zai Ya   Shong,   Mee Mee Yao Dei Shong   Hei Ya   Lee

14
S
A
T
B
Perc.
I
II
Pno. I
Pno. II
p sub.
f sub.
f sub.
p
(f)
f
Hei Ya Hei Ya Hei Ya Hei Ya Hei Ya Dei Shong,
Hei Ya Hei Ya Hei Ya Hei Ya Hei Ya Dei Shong,
Gu Gu Nao Zhai A Jou Zhai Ha. Hei Ya Hei Ya Mee Mee Hei Ya,
Gu Gu Nao Zhai A Jou Zhai Ha. Hei Ya Hei Ya Mee Mee Hei Ya,

18
S
Hei Ya Lee Dei Shong Hei Ya Lee Hei Ya Zhai Ha.
Shan Dan Dan Hua
A
Hei Ya Lee Dei Shong Hei Ya Lee Hei Ya Zhai Ha.
Shan Dan Dan Hua
T
Mee Mee Hei Ya Lee Hei Gu Gu Hei Ya Lee Hei.
Shan Dan Dan Hua
B
Mee Mee Hei Ya Lee Hei Gu Gu Hei Ya Lee Hei.
Shan Dan Dan Hua
Perc.
I
Small Tambourine
(buzz roll, snare drum stick)
II
Timp. solo
hard yarn mallet
(dead shot)
Pno. I
Pno. II

22
S
Kai, Hei Ya Lee Hei Ya Lee Hei Hei Hei Ya Lee Hei Hei Ya Lee Hei Ya Lee
A
Kai, Hei Ya Lee Hei Ya Lee Hei Hei Hei Ya Lee Hei Hei Ya Lee Hei Ya Lee
T
Kai, Hei Ya Lee Hei Hei Ya Lee Hei Hei Ya Lee Hei Ya Lee Hei
B
Kai, Hei Ya Lee Hei Hei Ya Lee Hei Hei Ya Lee Hei Ya Lee Hei
sim.
p
Perc.
I
II
Pno. I
mf
Pno. II
(Ped.)

27
S
Hei   Hei   Hei Ya Lee!   Shan Dan Hua,   Shan Dan Hua Kai,   Hei Ya Lee Hei,
A
Hei   Hei   Hei Ya Lee!   Shan Dan Hua,   Shan Dan Hua Kai,   Hei Ya Lee Hei,
T
Hei   Hei   Hei Ya Lee Hei!   Hei Ya   Hei Ya Lee Hei   Hei   Hei Ya, Shan   Dan Hua,
B
Hei   Hei   Hei Ya Lee Hei!   Hei Ya   Hei Ya Lee Hei   Hei   Hei Ya, Shan   Dan Hua,
Perc.
I
Sm. Tamb.
II
Timp. +
Pno. I
Pno. II
molto

32
S
Shan Dan Hua Kai, Hei Ya Lee Hei Hei Ya Lee Hei Hei Ya Lee Hei Ya Lee
(ppp)
p
A
Shan Dan Hua Kai, Hei Ya Lee Hei Hei Ya Lee Hei Hei Ya Lee Hei Ya Lee
(ppp)
p
T
Hei Ya Lee Hei Ya Lee Hei Hei Ya, Shan Dan Hua, Hei Ya Lee Hei Ya Lee Hei
(ppp)
p
B
Hei Ya Lee Hei Ya Lee Hei Hei Ya, Shan Dan Hua, Hei Ya Lee Hei Ya Lee Hei
(ppp)
p
Perc.
I
II
Timp. solo
hard yarn mallet
f
ff
Pno. I
f
fff
fff
Pno. II
ff

35
S
A
T
B
Perc.
I
II
Pno. I
Pno. II
Sm. Tamb.
8va
Hei Hei Hei Ya Lee Hei Hei Ya Lee Hei Hei Ya Lee Hei Ya
Hei Hei Hei Ya Lee Hei Hei Ya Lee Hei Hei Ya Lee Shan Dan Dan Hua Ya
Hei Hei Hei Ya Lee Hei Hei Ya Lee Hei Hei Ya Lee Shan Dan Dan Hua Ya
Hei Hei Hei Ya Lee Hei Hei Ya Lee Hei Hei Ya Lee Hei Ya

38
S
Hei   Hei Ya Hei _______ Ya   Hei Ya Lee Hei Hei   Hei Ya Lee Hei Hei
A
Kai Zai _ Ya _____ Shong, Gu Gu Nee Zhai ____ Ha
T
Kai Zai _ Ya ____ Shong Mee Mee Nee Dei ____ Shong,
B
Hei   Hei Ya Hei _______ Ya   Hei Ya Lee Hei Hei   Hei Ya Lee Hei Ya Lee
Perc.
I
II
Pno. I
Pno. II
sim.

Hei Hei Hei Hei Ya Lee Hei Hei Hei Ya Lee Hei Hei Hei Hei Hei Hei Ya
Hei Ya Hei Ya Hei Hei Hei Hei, Hei Ya Lee Hei Ya Lee Hei Ya Hei Hei Hei Hei Ya

S
A
T
B
Perc.
Pno. I
Pno. II
46
ff
ff
sfp
(p)
Lee.
Gu _ Gu Nee Zhai _ Ha, _
ff
ff
sfp
Gu _ Gu Nee Zhai _ Ha, _
ff
sfp
(p)
Mee _ Mee Nee Dei _ Shong _
(p)
ff
ff
sfp
Lee
Mee _ Mee Nee Dei _ Shong _
Sm. Tamb.
sim.
f
Timp.
sim.
mf
8va
f
sim.
sim.
ff
fff
sim.
sim.

50
50A
50B
51
ff
ppp sub.
S
A
T
B
A,
A,
A,
A,
(Sm. Tamb.)
Perc.
(Timp.)
I
II
(f)
ff
Solo
(mf)
f
Pno. I
(f)
fff
Pno. II
(fff)

52
f rhythmic
S
Shan Dan Dan Hua Kai Zai Ya Shong Kai Zai Ya Shong Kai Zai Ya Shong
f rhythmic
A
Shan Dan Dan Hua Kai Zai Ya Shong Kai Zai Ya Shong Kai Zai Ya Shong
f rhythmic
T
Shan Dan Hua Kai Shan Dan Hua Kai Hei Ya Lee Shan Dan Hua Kai Hei Ya
f rhythmic
B
Shan Dan Hua Kai Shan Dan Hua Kai Hei Ya Lee Shan Dan Hua Kai Hei Ya
I
Perc.
II
8va.
Pno. I
Pno. II

56
S
Kai __ Zai Ya __ Shong, Shan __ Dan Dan Hua Shan _ Dan Dan Hua Kai _ Zai Ya _
A
Kai Zai Ya __ Shong, Hei Hei Hei Hei Hei Hei Hei
T
Shan Dan Hua Kai Zai Ya _ Shong Hei Hei Hei Hei Hei Ya Lee
B
Shan __ Dan Hua Kai, Hei Hei Hei Hei Hei Ya Lee
più f
(f) cresc.
f cresc.
ff
8va
Perc.
I
II
Pno. I
Pno. II

60
S
Zai Ya Shong, Hei Ya Hei Hei Ya Hei Hei Ya
A
Hei Hei Hei Hei Ya Hei Hei Ya Hei Hei Ya
T
Hei Ya Lee Hei Hei Hei Shan Dan Dan Hua Kai Zai Ya Shong,
B
Hei Ya Lee Hei Hei Hei Shan Dan Dan Hua Kai Zai Ya Shong,
Perc.
I
II
Pno. I
8va
Pno. II

64
sim.
pp sub.
Hei Ya Lee Hei Ya Lee Hei Shan Dan Dan Hua Kai,
sim.
pp sub.
Hei Ya Lee Hei Ya Lee Hei Shan Dan Dan Hua Shan Dan Dan
Shan Dan Hua Kai Zai Ya Shong, Shan Dan Hua Kai Zai Ya Shong,
pp sub.
Shan Dan Hua Kai Zai Ya Shong, Shan Dan Dan Hua Kai Zai Ya
I
Perc.
II
8va
sim.
Pno. I
pp sub.
fff
sim.
Pno. II
(ff) fff
pp sub.
sim.

68
S
Shan _ Dan Dan Hua,   Shan _ Dan Dan Hua _ Kai,   Shan _ Dan Dan Hua _ Kai, Shan _
(pp) cresc.
A
Hua _ Kai Zai Ya _ Shong,   Shan _ Dan _ Dan _ Hua Kai   Shan Dan Dan
(pp) cresc.
T
Hua Kai Zai _______ Ya Shong,   Shan _ Dan Dan Hua Kai Zai Ya _ Shong,
(pp) cresc.
B
Shong,   Kai _ Zai   Kai Zai _____ Kai _ Zai Ya _ Shong,   Shan Dan Dan
(pp)   cresc.
Perc.
I (Sm. Tamb.)
mp   mp
II (Timp.)
mf   mf
Pno. I
8va
(pp) (pp) cresc.
(pp)
(fff) (fff)
Pno. II
(pp) cresc.

72
(cresc.)
fff
S
Dan Dan Hua Kai Zai Ya _ Shong, Shan _ Dan _ Dan _ Hua Kai _ Zai Kai _ Zai _ Ya _ Shong,
(cresc.)
fff
A
Hua _ Kai Zai Ya _ Shong, Shan Dan _ Dan Hua _ Kai Hua _ Kai Zai _____ Ya Shong,
(cresc.)
fff
T
Shan Dan Dan _ Hua Kai _ Zai Ya _ Shong Shan Dan _ Dan Hua Kai _ Zai _____ Ya _ Shong,
(cresc.)
fff
I
B
Hua Kai _ Zai Ya Shong, Shan _ Dan Dan Hua _ Shan Dan Dan Hua _ Kai Zai _ Ya Shong,
(cresc.)
fff
II
Hua Kai _ Zai Ya Shong, Shan _ Dan Dan Hua _ Shan Dan Dan Hua _ Kai Zai _ Ya Shong,
(Sm. Tamb.)
I
Perc.
mf
ff
(Timp.)
II
f
ff
8va
mp cresc.
Pno. I
fff
mp cresc.
Pno. II
fff

*Glissando at the very end of the first note value.

**Here the second piano should not play if the chorus has no difficulty finding the pitches.

II. A Pair of Mules
(Homage to Ferde Grofé)

一對騾子

* The chorus should be divided into six equally balanced sections.
** Pno. I: Grace notes always *on* the beat.
*** Pno. II: Grace notes always *before* the beat.

5
S
M
A
T
Bar.
B
Perc.
I
II
(W. Blks.)
Pno. I
Pno. II
Yee Dui Dee Ma
Yo Luo
Yee Dui Dee Ma Jou,
Lou Zi Zhe Luo
Yo
Yo
pp
pp
pp
pp
pp
p
p
pp
mp
mp
mf
p

♩ = 52
rit.
♩ = 50
9
S
mp
pp
Jou,
M
mp
mfp
pp
pp
(non cresc.)
Zi
Zhe,
Luo
Zi
A
mf
sub.
pp
(pp)
(non cresc.)
Zou
Ning Xia Yo,
Luo
Zi
T
mp
mfp
pp
Zi
Zhe,
Bar.
p
mf
pp
Tuo
Yee Kun Ma Yo,
B
p
mf
pp
Yee
Kun
Ma,
Perc.
I
II
Pno. I
p
pp
mp
Pno. II
pp
mp
p
pp
3
p
pp

* The chorus should now be divided into four equally balanced sections.

rit.
♩ = 52
17
S
A
T
B
Zi _ Zhe, Luo _ Zi _ Zhe.
Luo Zi _ Zhe _ Yo.
Zhe, Luo _ Zi _ Zhe, _ Zou _ Ning _ Xia Yo.
_ Luo Zi _ Zhe. _ Yee
pp
p pp
(f) pp
pp pp (non cresc.)
Perc.
I
II
W. Blks.
pp
3 3
Pno. I
mf (mf)
mf
pp
3 3 3
mf p
Pno. II
p
p mp
3
3 3 3
pp

21
S
Yee Dui Dee Ma Jou Luo Zi
A
Yee Dui Luo Zi Zhe, Zuo Ning Xia Yo,
T
Yee Dui Dee Ma Jou Luo Zi Zhe, Yee Dui Dee Ma Jou
B
Dui Dee Luo Zi Zhe, Zuo Ning
Perc.
I
II
Pno. I
Pno. II

25
S
Zhe, Yee Dui Dee Ma Jou Luo Zi Zhe,
A
Zuo Ning Xia Yo, Yo,
T
Luo Zi Zhe, Zuo Ning Xia Yo, Yee Dui
B
Xia, Yee Dui Dee Ma Jou Luo Zi Zhe, Zuo
Perc.
I
II
Pno. I
Pno. II

Yee Dui Dee Ma Jou Luo Zi Zhe, Yee Dui Dee Luo Zi Zhe,
Yee Dui Dee Ma Jou Luo Zi Zhe, Yee Dui Dee Luo Zi
Yee Dui Dee Ma Jou Luo Zi Zhe, Yee Dui Dee Luo Zi
Yee Dui Dee Ma Jou Luo Zi Zhe, Yee Dui Dee
Yo, Zuo Ning Xia Yo,
Dee Ma Jou Luo Zi Zhe, Yee
Ning Xia Lou Zi Zhe, Yee
Ning Xia Yo,

31
S
I
M
II
A
T
I
Bar.
II
B
Perc.
I
II
Marimba (hard mallets)
Pno. I
Pno. II
Yee Dui Dee Luo Zi, Yee Dui Dee
Zhe, Yee Dui Dee Luo Zi, Yee Dui Dee
Zhe, Yee Dui Dee, Yee Dui Dee Luo Zi
Luo Zi Zhe, Yee Dui Dee, Yee Dui Dee Luo Zi
Yee Dui Luo Zi, Yee Dui Dee Luo Zi Yo, Luo
Dui Dee Luo Zi Zhe, Yee Dui, Yee Dui Dee Luo Zi Yo, Luo
Dui Dee Luo Zi Zhe, Yee Dui, Dee Luo Zi Zhe, Luo
Yee Dui, Yee Dui, Dee Luo Zi Zhe, Luo

33 (mp)
S
Luo Zi Zhe Ya Ya Ha Ha Ha Ya
A
Zhe, Luo Zi Zhe Ya Ya Ha Ha Ha Ya
T
Zi Yo, Luo Zi Yo, Yee Dui Dee Luo Zi Zhe,
B
Zi Yo, Yee Dui Dee Luo Zi Zhe, Luo Zi Zhe,
I
Perc.
(Mar.)
II
p
mf mf
Pno. I
mp cresc.
3
f p
ff
3
Pno. II
3
mf
3
mf
p f

TWO FOLK SONGS FROM QINGHAI

I. Morningstar Lily
(Homage to Igor Stravinsky)

Bright Sheng
(1990)

* Although this part is used by both players, we have included two versions of it
  with slightly different layouts to facilitate page turns for each percussionist.

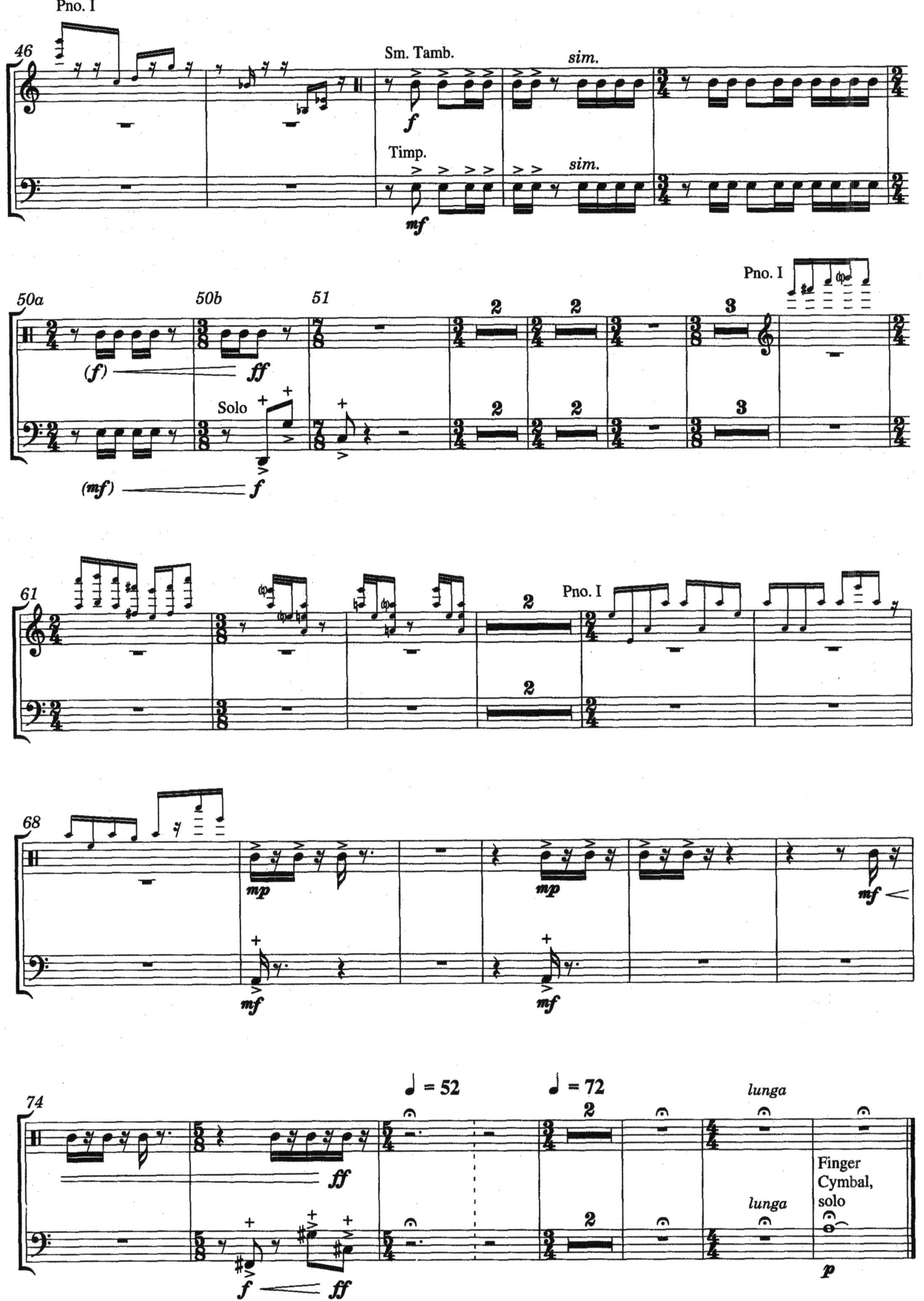
Pno. I
46
Sm. Tamb.
sim.
f
Timp.
sim.
mf
50a
50b
51
2
2
3
Pno. I
(f)
ff
Solo
2
2
3
(mf)
f
61
Pno. I
2
2
68
mp
mp
mf
mf
mf
74
♩ = 52
♩ = 72
lunga
2
ff
lunga
Finger
Cymbal,
solo
2
f
ff
p

II. A Pair of Mules
(Homage to Ferde Grofé)

Percussion I

78
(W. Blks.)
(Crot.)
(Mar.)
p
82
(W. Blks.)
Crot.
(mf)
p
(Mar.)
(mp)
85
(W. Blks.)
W. Blks.
p sub.
(Crot.)
(Mar.)
cresc.
mp
Mar.
mf
mp
88
(W. Blks.)
mf
(Crot.)
cresc.
(Mar.)
(mf)
(f)
f
ff
f
ff

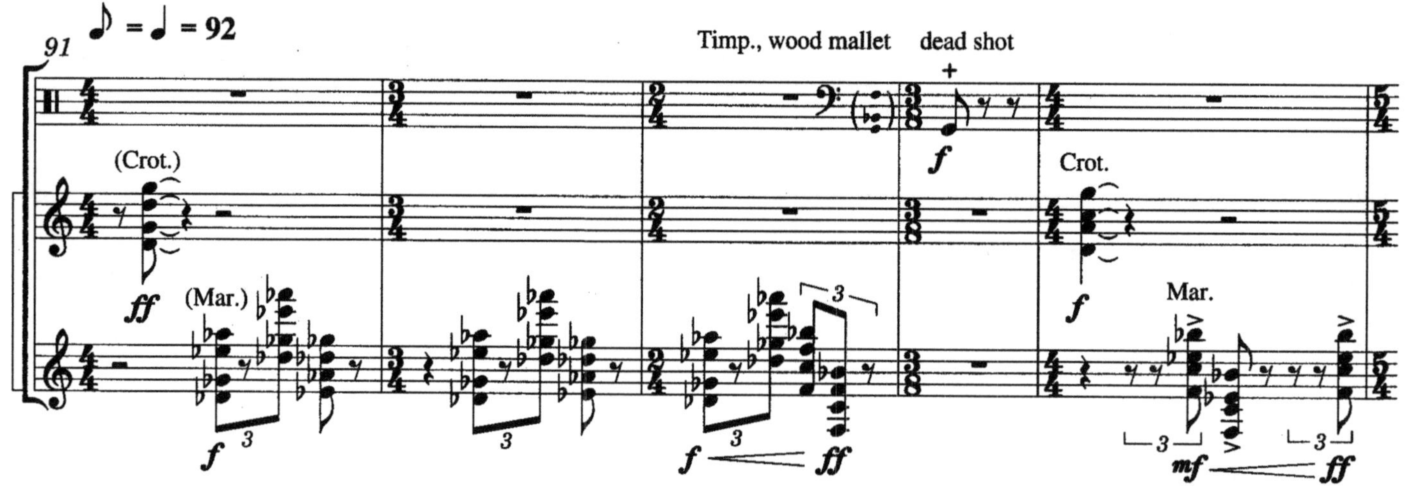
91
♪ = ♩ = 92
Timp., wood mallet   dead shot
(Crot.)
ff   (Mar.)
f
Crot.
f
Mar.
mf   ff

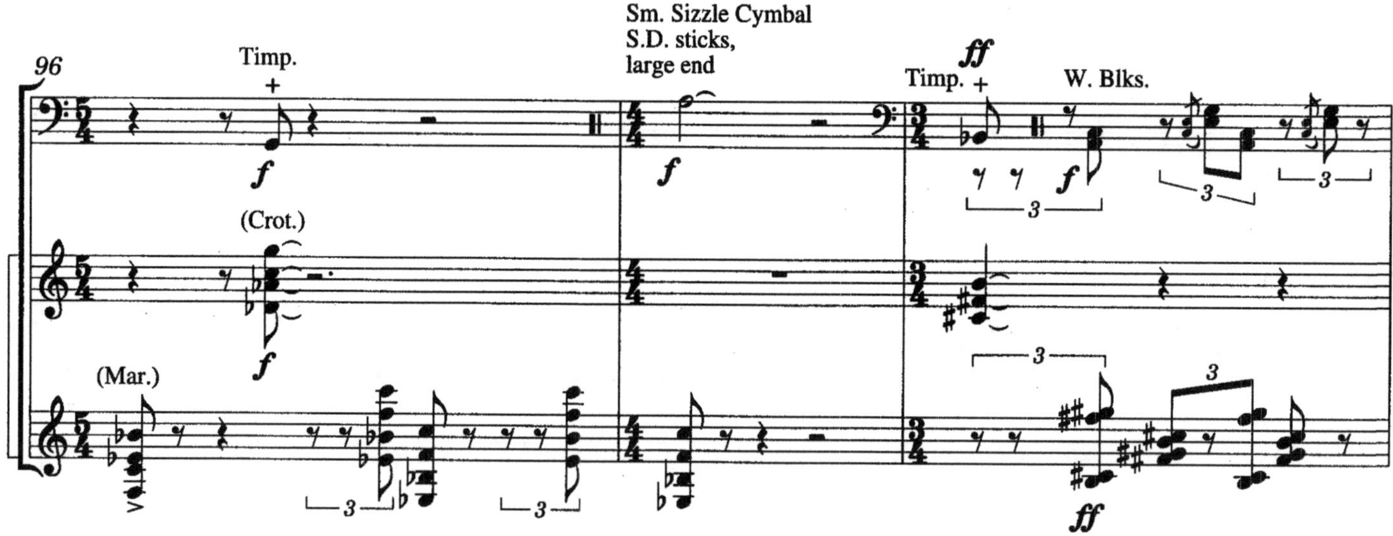
96
Timp.
Sm. Sizzle Cymbal
S.D. sticks,
large end
Timp.   ff   W. Blks.
f
f
f
(Crot.)
f
(Mar.)
ff

99   (W. Blks.)
Mar.

102 (W. Blks.)
(Mar.)
(ff)
fff
3

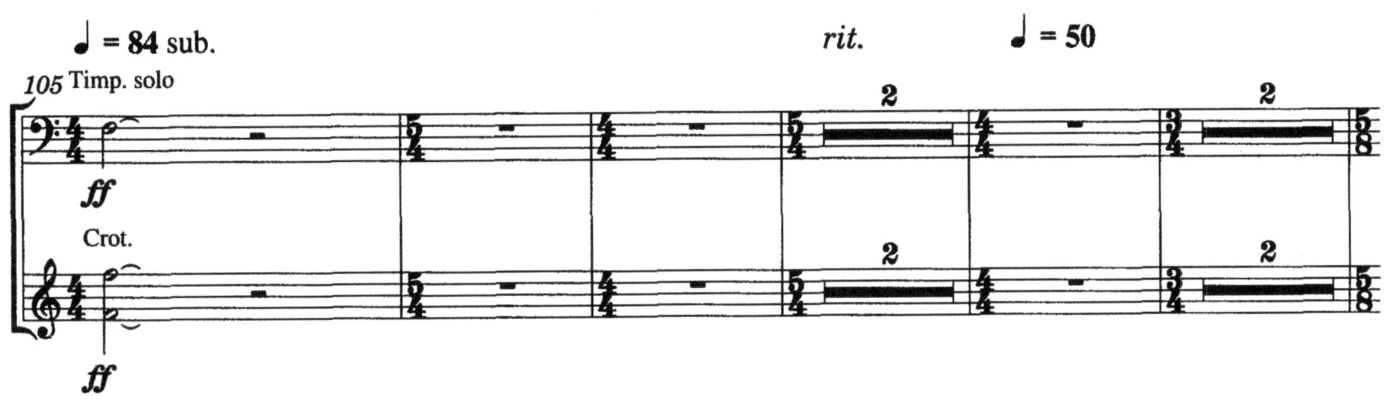
♩ = 84 sub.
rit.
♩ = 50
105 Timp. solo
ff
Crot.
ff

113

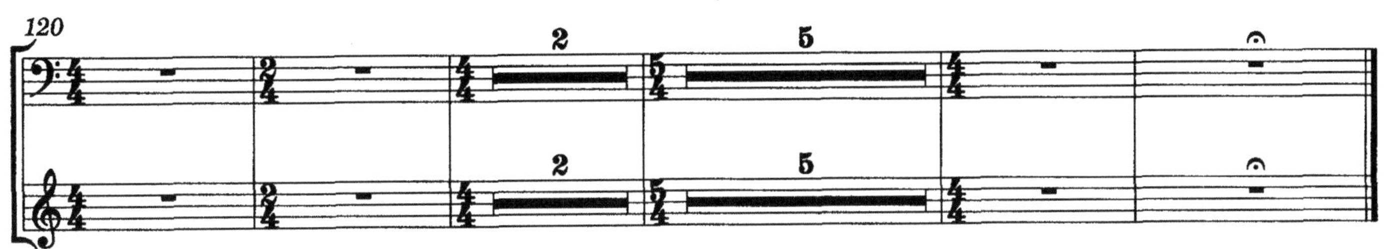
120

TWO FOLK SONGS FROM QINGHAI

I. Morningstar Lily
(Homage to Igor Stravinsky)

Bright Sheng
(1990)

* Although this part is used by both players, we have included two versions of it
  with slightly different layouts to facilitate page turns for each percussionist.

Pno. I
46
Sm. Tamb.
sim.
Timp.
sim.
f
mf
50a
50b
51
Pno. I
(f)
ff
Solo
(mf)
f
2
2
3
61
Pno. I
2
2
68
mp
mp
mf
mf
mf
74
= 52
= 72
lunga
ff
Finger
Cymbal,
solo
lunga
2
f
ff
p

II. A Pair of Mules
(Homage to Ferde Grofé)

Wood Blocks
solo
40
Crot.
ppp
ppp
46 (W. Blks.)
(2 + 3)
(Crot.)
(ppp)
(ppp)
51 (W. Blks.)
7
solo
Crot.
7
p
63 (W. Blks.)
(p)
Crot.
pp
69 W. Blks.
pp
Crot.
74 (W. Blks.)
I
mf
(pp)
(Crot.)
p
Mar.
hard mallet
II
pp

78 (W. Blks.)
(Crot.)
(Mar.)
p
3
82 (W. Blks.)
(Mar.)
(mp)
Crot.
(mf)
p
85 (W. Blks.)
W. Blks.
p sub.
(Crot.)
(Mar.)
mf
cresc.
Mar.
mp
mp
88 (W. Blks.)
mf
(Crot.)
cresc.
(Mar.)
(f)
ff
f
(mf)
f
ff

91
♪ = ♩ = 92
Timp., wood mallet   dead shot
(Crot.)
f
Crot.
ff
(Mar.)
f
Mar.
f
mf
ff

96
Timp.
f
Sm. Sizzle Cymbal
S.D. sticks,
large end
f
Timp.
ff
W. Blks.
f
(Crot.)
f
(Mar.)
ff

99 (W. Blks.)
Mar.

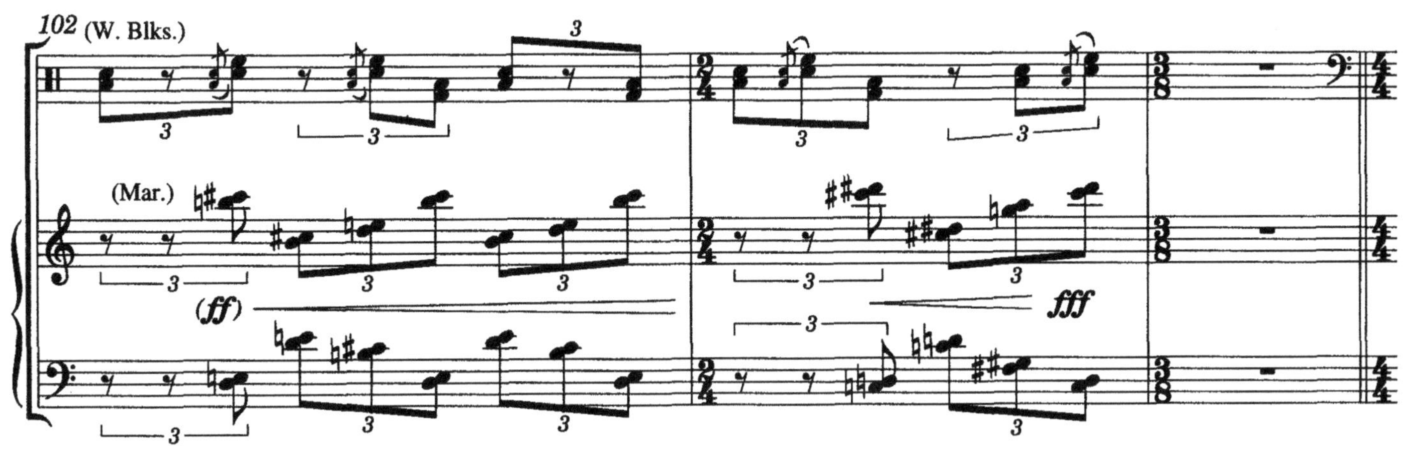
102 (W. Blks.)
(Mar.)
(ff)
fff

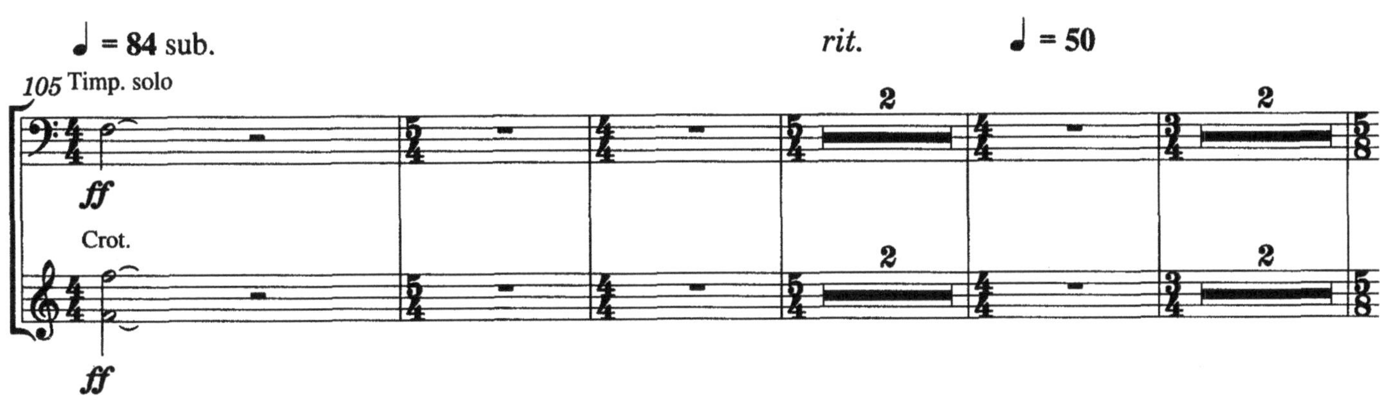
♩ = 84 sub.
rit.
♩ = 50
105 Timp. solo
ff
Crot.
ff

113

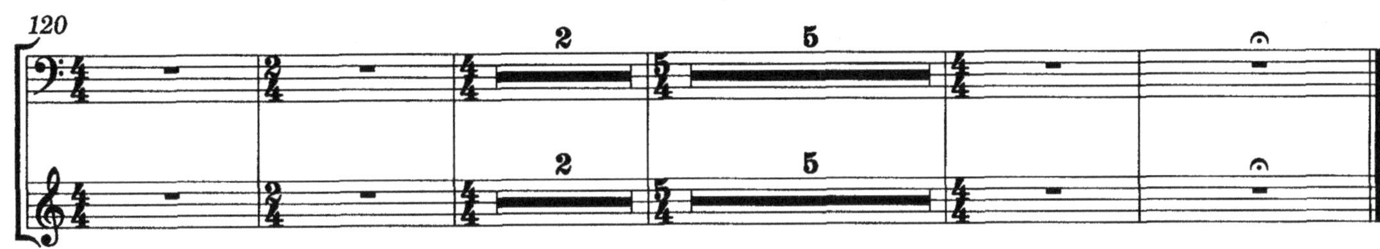
120

35
fffp
S
Yo,
fffp
A
Yo,
T
ff
Zou
Ning Xia Yo.
B
ff
Luo
Zi Yo.
I
(Mar.)
Perc.
mp
mf
mf
mp
mf
II
Pno. I
mf
cresc.
Pno. II
p
3
f
3
f
mf
f
mf
f

♩ = 92
38
fff
(6")
p dolce
S
Yee   Dui Dee Ma Jou Lou Zi __ Zhe,
fff
(6")
pp dolce e legato
A
Yo,
(ff)   fff   (6")
T
(ff)   fff   (6")
B
Crotales   solo   (6")
I
p
ppp
(Mar.)   (6")
Perc.
II
f
ff
p
(6")
(cresc.)   ff   fff   pp
Pno. I
(6")
(f)   fff
Pno. II

42
S
Zou Dee Ning Xia Yo, Tuo Ei Yee Kun Ma Yo, Hui Lai Shi Ma Jou
A
Yo, Yo, Yo,
T
pp dolce e legato
Yo,
B
Perc.
I
(Crot.)
II
Wood Blocks solo
ppp
3 3 3 3 3 3
Pno. I
8va
loco
p
pp
p
Pno. II

47
(2 + 3)
S
Shao Liao Dai Zao Ya Ha Jou Er, Dian Dian Hua Er Kai
A
p
Yo, Yee Dui
T
B
Perc.
(Crot.)
I
(W. Blks.)
II
(ppp) (ppp)
3 3 3 3 3
Pno. I
(2 + 3)
pp (pp) mf
Pno. II
(2 + 3)

51
S
A
T
B
Ya Yo.
Yo,
Dee Ma Jou Luo Zi Zhe, Zuo Dee Ning Xia Yo, Tuo Ei
pp
Yo, Yo, Yo,
Perc.
I
(Crot.)
II
(W. Blks.)
3
3
Pno. I
mp
Pno. II
p
3
(p)
3
f
p

55
S
A
T
B
Perc.
I
II
Pno. I
Pno. II
Yo,
Yo,
Yee Kun Ma Yo, Hui Lai Shi Ma Jou Shao Liao Dai, Zao Ya
Yo, Yo, Yo,
Yee Dui Dee Luo Zi Zhe, Zou Dee Ning
mp
(mp)
p
ff
p
3
3
3

59
S
A
T
B
Perc.
I
II
Pno. I
Pno. II
Ha Jou Er, Dian Dian Hua Er Kai Ya Yo.
Yee Dui Dee Luo
Xia Yo, Tuo Ei Yee Kun Ma Yo,
ff sub.
pp
W. Blks.
solo
pp
3
3
pp
f
(p)
mf
ff
p
f
3
3
3

63
S
A
f
Yo,
Yo,
Yo,
T
Zi Zhe Zou Dee Ning Xia, Hui Lai Shi Ma Jou Shao Liao
B
mp
mf
Hui Lai Shi Shao Liao Dai Zao Er, Dian Dian Hua Er
Perc.
I
W. Blks.
(pp) 3
3 3 3 3 3
II
Pno. I
ff p ff pp f
Pno. II
3 p mf
p p
3 3 3 3
3 3
mp

66
S
I
M
II
A
T
B
Yee Dui Luo Zi Zhe Zou Ning Xia Yo.
Yee Dui Luo Zi Zhe Zou Ning Zou Dee Ning Xia Yo.
Yee Dui Dee Luo Zi Zhe, Zou Dee Ning Xia Yo.
Yee Dui Dee Luo Zi Zhe, Zou Ning Xia
Dai. Yee Dui Dee Luo Zi Zhe, Zou Ning Xia
Kai Ya Yo.
(W. Blks.)
Perc.
I
II
3
(Crot.)
mp
8va
loco
Pno. I
p
(p)
mp
mf
p
mf
Pno. II
3
3
3
3
3
3
mp
p
mp

70
S
M
A
T
Bar.
B
Perc. I
Perc. II
Pno. I
Pno. II
f
Luo Zi Zhe.
p!
Luo Zi
p (p!)
Yo. Yee Dui Ma Jou Luo Zi Zhe Yee Dui Luo Zi
p f sub.
Yo. Yee Dui Dee Luo Zi Zhe Zou Ning Xia
f
Yee Dui Dee Ma Jou Luo Zi Zhe
f
Yee Dui Dee Ma Jou Luo Zi Zhe
(W. Blks.)
pp 3 3 3 3 3
(Crot.)
(pp)
f p mp
p 3 3 3 3 3
(p) (p) sim.
mf 3
p
3 3

73
(f)
S
M
A
T
Bar.
B
Perc.
Pno. I
Pno. II
Yee Dui
Zhe.
Yee Dui
(p) cresc.
Luo Zi Zou Ning Xia, Yee Dui Dee Ma Jou Luo Zi Zhe,
Zou Ning Xia Yo, Yee Dui Dee Ma Jou Luo Zi Zhe,
Zou Ning Xia Hui Lai Shi Ma Jou,
Zou Ning Xia Hui Lai Shi Ma Jou,
(W. Blks.)
3 3 3 3 3 3 3
(Crot.)
(pp)
p
p mp
(sim.) sim.
p p mp mf
3 3 3 3
f
f

76
S: Dee Ma Jou Luo Zi Zhe.
M: Dee Ma Jou Luo Zi Zhe.
(cresc.)
A: Yee Dui Dee Luo Zi Zou Ning Xia Yo,
f
T: Zou Ning Xia Yo, Zou Ning Xia Yo,
Bar.: Shao Liao Dai Zao Er, Yee
B: Shao Liao Dai Zao Er, Yee
Perc.
I (W. Blks.)
mf
II (Crot.)
Mar. (hard mallet)
pp
p
Pno. I
Pno. II
mf

79
S
M
A
T
Bar.
I
II
B
Perc.
I
II
Pno. I
Pno. II
Yo, Yo, Yo, Yo,
Zou Ning Xia Yo, Yee Dui Dee
f
Luo Zi Zhe, Luo Zi Yo,
f
Luo Zi Zhe, Luo Zi Zhe, Luo
Dui Luo Zi Zhe, Yee Dui Ma Jou Luo Zi Zhe, Luo
Dui Luo Zi Zhe, Yee Dui Ma Jou Luo Zi Zhe, Luo
Dui Luo Zi Zhe, Yee Dui Ma Jou Luo Zi Zhe, Luo
(W. Blks.)
(Crot.)
(Mar.)
cresc.

82
(f)
ff
S
Yee Dui Ma Jou Luo Zi Zhe, Luo
(f)
ff
I
Luo Zi Yo, Yee Dui Ma Jou Luo Zi Zhe, Luo
M
(f) f cresc.
II
Luo Zi Yo, Yee Diu Dee Luo Zi Zhe, Luo
(f) cresc.
A
Luo Zi Yo, Yee Diu Dee Luo Zi Zhe, Luo
(f) ff
T
Zi Zhe Zou Ning Xia Yo, Luo Zi
(f) ff ff
B
Zi Zhe Yo, Yo, Luo Zi Zhe,
(W. Blks.)
I
3 3 3 3 3 3 (mf)
Perc.
Crot.
II
p
(Mar.)
3 3 3 3 3 3 3 3
(mp)
3 3 3 3
Pno. I
(cresc.) 3 3
3 3
(mf)
Pno. II
f
3 3

85
S
I
M
II
A
T
B
Perc.
I
II
Pno. I
Pno. II
(ff)
sub. p
cresc.
Zi Zhe, Ma Jou Ma Jou, Ma
ff
sub. p
cresc.
Zi Zhe, Ma Jou Ma Jou, Ma
sub. p
cresc.
Zi Ma Jou Ma Jou, Ma
ff
molto
sub. p
cresc.
Zi Zhe, Ma Jou Ma Jou, Ma
(ff)
p
cresc.
Zhe, Luo Zi Zhe, Ma Jou Ma Jou, Ma
(ff)
(ff)
Luo Zi Zhe
(W. Blks.)
p sub.
3 3 3 3 3 3
(Crot.)
(Mar.)
mf
3
ff
3
pp
ff
ff
p

87
S
M
A
T
Bar.
B
Perc.
Pno. I
Pno. II
Jou, Ma Jou, Ma Jou, Ma Jou,
Jou, Ma Jou, Ma Jou,
Jou, Ma Jou, Ma Jou, Yee Dui Dee Luo Zi
Jou, Ma Jou, Ma Jou, Yee Dui Dee Luo Zi
Yee Dui Dee Ma
Yee Dui Dee Ma
(W. Blks.)
(Crot.)
(Mar.)
I
II
cresc.
mp
mf
p
mp
f

89
S
Ma Jou, Ma
M
Ma Jou, Ma
A
Zhe, Ma
T
Zhe, Ma
Bar.
Jou, Ma
B
Jou, Ma
Perc.
(W. Blks.)
(cresc.) (Crot.)
(Mar.)
Pno. I
Pno. II

48

93
(fff)
(fff)
(fff)
(fff)
S
A
T
B
Perc.
I
II
Timp., wood mallet
dead shot
+
f
(Mar.)
3
3
f
ff
Pno. I
8va
3
3
3
3
3
3
(ff)
p sub.
Ped.
Pno. II
3
3
3
3
(ff)
fff
Ped.

95
ff
S
Ma
ff
A
Ma
ff
T
Ma
ff
B
Ma
Perc.
I
II
(Crot.)
f
(Mar.)
mf
ff
8
ff
ff
8va.
Pno. I
fff
ff
(Ped.)
Pno. II
fff
pp sub.
Ped.
3

Jou.
Jou.
Jou.
Jou.
(Timp.)
(Crot.)
(Mar.)
8va
8va

52
97
fff
S
A
T
B
Sm. Sizzle Cymbal
S.D. sticks, bigger end
f
Perc.
I
(Mar.)
II
8va
Pno. I
3
p sub.
Ped.
Pno. II
ff
(Ped.)

98
ff
S
Ma Jou Yo, Ma
A
ff
Ma Jou Yo, Ma
T
ff
Ma Jou, Ma Jou,
B
ff
Ma Jou, Ma Jou,
Perc.
(Timp.) ff W. Blks.
I
3 f 3 3 3 3
(Crot.)
II
3 3 3
(Mar.)
ff
Pno. I
3
fff ff 3 3
3
Pno. II
f tr tr tr tr
tr tr

100
S
A
T
B
(ff)
(ff)
(ff)
(ff)
Jou
Yo.
Jou
Yo.
Yo
Yo.
Yo
Yo.
(W. Blks.)
Perc.
I
II
(Mar.)
Pno. I
Pno. II
ff
sfp
3
3
3
3
3
3
3
3
3
3
3
3

101
S
A
T
B
(W. Blks.)
I
(Mar.)
Perc.
II
(ff)
Pno. I
Pno. II
fff

103
fff
fff
fff
fff
S
A
T
B
(W. Blks.)
(Mar.)
Perc.
I
II
fff
Pno. I
mf sub.
Ped.
Pno. II
ff
fff
Ped.

= 84 sub.
rit.
105
fff
(fff)
S
Luo
Zi
Zhe.
fff
(fff)
A
Luo
Zi
Zhe.
fff
(fff)
T
Luo
Zi
Zhe.
fff
(fff)
B
Luo
Zi
Zhe.
Timp. solo
I
ff
Perc.
Crot.
II
ff
Pno. I
fff
fff
(Ped.)
8va
Pno. II
fff
fff
Ped.
Ped.

110
♩ = 50
ppp sempre
Ma _____ Jou. Ma _____ Jou. Ma _____ Jou._
ppp sempre
Ma _____ Jou, _____ Jou._
ppp
pp ppp sempre
Ma _____ Jou._
ppp
Ma _____ Jou. _____ Zou _____
pp
S
A
T
B
Perc.
I
II
Pno. I
Pno. II

116
S
A
T
B
Yee   Dui   Dee   Ma   Jou.
Ma   Jou.
Ning Xia   Yo.
Perc.
I
II
Pno. I
Pno. II

121
S
A
T
Yo.
B
Yo.
Perc.
W. Blk., solo
3
pp
3
3
I
Crot., solo
p
II
Pno. I
ff
p
Pno. II
8va
pp molto legato
p
3
3
ff
(ff) > mf
pp
ff
(ff)
ppp

126
S
A
T
B
Perc.
I
II
Pno. I
Pno. II
pppp
pppp
pppp
pppp
fff
ppp
8
pp